Original title:
Obsidian Dams Amid the Mermaid Cap

Author: Olivia Oja
ISBN HARDBACK: 978-1-80562-347-2
ISBN PAPERBACK: 978-1-80563-868-1

The Lure of the Midnight Abyss

In shadows deep where phantoms tread,
A whisper calls, the brave are led.
The moonlight dances on the brim,
Of secrets kept, and dreams grown dim.

Beneath the waves, a siren sings,
Of treasures lost and broken wings.
The night unfolds, a velvet cloak,
Where every breath feels like a joke.

With every glance, the darkness grows,
For what it hides, no heart yet knows.
The waters churn with ancient lore,
An endless ache, a fateful shore.

The stars above begin to fade,
As restless souls in silence wade.
To dive or not, the choice is clear,
But can we face what we most fear?

So take my hand, let shadows play,
And together we'll drift far away.
Into the depths, where whispers twine,
In the midnight abyss, fate's design.

Whispered Secrets of Drowning Stars

In twilight's glow, the starlit sink,
A cosmic realm makes dreamers think.
Each twinkle hides a tale untold,
Of love and loss, of hearts turned cold.

The void expands, a breath so light,
While constellations hold us tight.
With every pulse, a truth revealed,
The mysteries of night unsealed.

A comet streaks, its shimmer fades,
And in that flash, a world cascades.
The echoes of a million cries,
Float softly through the velvet skies.

We chase the light, lest shadows creep,
Through realms we wander, lost in sleep.
With every wish upon a star,
We grasp the dreams that feel so far.

Yet whispered secrets cling like dew,
To hearts that dare to seek the true.
In every spark, a tale we share,
Of drowning stars and silent prayer.

Dances of the Abyssal Song

In depths where shadows twist and twine,
The echoes sing of lost design.
With whispers soft like siren calls,
The water's breath in twilight falls.

Beneath the waves, where secrets lie,
The ancient songs take to the sky.
Each note a ripple, soft and clear,
That draws the brave, yet chills with fear.

Glimmers flash like fleeting dreams,
In currents deep where nothing seems.
An ocean's heart beats wild and vast,
While shadows dance, the die is cast.

As winds entwine with scented sea,
The melody flows wild and free.
In every surge, a tale retold,
Of treasures lost and legends bold.

Yet still we yearn for what is near,
The vibrant notes, the distant sphere.
In abyssal depths, we find our fate,
A haunting song that won't abate.

Shadows Over Shimmering Waters

Upon the lake, where ripples kiss,
The golden hues of twilight bliss.
Shadows drift like echoes cast,
In shimmering tales of moments past.

The moonlight dances on the waves,
In secret paths where silence saves.
Each splash a whisper, soft and light,
That beckons dreams and fades from sight.

Yet in the depths, a story brews,
Of forgotten hopes and timeless blues.
Beneath the stars, the water calls,
It wraps around, as nature sprawls.

With every breeze, the secrets swell,
In twilight's hush, they weave their spell.
The shadows over waters bright,
Hold mysteries wrapped in gentle night.

And as we gaze with yearning eyes,
The shimmering truth beneath the skies.
We dance upon this enchanted shore,
Where every breath reveals much more.

Beneath the Gaze of Moonlit Dreams

Under the moon's soft silver glow,
The secrets of the night bestow.
With whispers low, the shadows creep,
And cradle soft the dreams we keep.

In silence deep, the stars awake,
To weave a fate we dare not break.
Each twinkle sings a lullaby,
That lifts our souls to wander high.

The world beneath, a canvas dark,
Invites the light to leave its mark.
In whispered tones, the night reveals,
The magic spun in midnight steals.

As visions dance upon the dawn,
We learn the truths that keep us drawn.
Beneath the gaze of dreams we trust,
We find our path, awakened, just.

In fragile moments, time stands still,
As dreams awaken in the chill.
A tapestry of night unfolds,
Beneath the moon, our heart's true holds.

Where the Tide Meets the Hidden Stone

At the shore where waters meet,
The whispers gather, soft and sweet.
Tidal secrets, ancient plans,
Lay beneath the sun-bleached sands.

With every wave that crashes near,
A tale emerges crystal clear.
In foamy rides, a journey calls,
As the ocean weaves, and silence falls.

Hidden stones beneath the tide,
Guard the treasures long denied.
Each glance reveals a world once lost,
Rekindled dreams, a heartfelt cost.

And there, where ocean’s pulse aligns,
Life dances in the briny pines.
The tide can tell of love's embrace,
Of whispered sighs that time can't trace.

Yet in the depths, we seek to know,
The secrets held in ebb and flow.
For where the tide gives way to stone,
The heart remembers, never alone.

Secrets Carved in Marine Stone

In the depths where shadows tread,
Whispers of the ocean's thread.
Fables etched on ancient slate,
Guardians of a hidden fate.

Bubbles rise from secrets kept,
Where mermaids once have softly wept.
Coral scripts that tales unfold,
Of sunken ships and treasures old.

Mysteries in the briny deep,
Where echoes of the past do sleep.
Fathoms wide, a heart does yearn,
For stories lost that still return.

Waves sing songs of love and loss,
Crashing dreams beneath the gloss.
Each tide pulls at the heart's desire,
Sparks of hope, like seashell fire.

With every dawn, new paths are drawn,
In the twilight, the old is gone.
Secrets linger, ever near,
In the whispers only waters hear.

Ethereal Dwellings of Forgotten Lore

In realms unseen where soft lights play,
Whispers of old stories sway.
Winds of magic dance through trees,
Calling forth the ancient seas.

Hollow trunks and mossy stones,
Carry tales of long-lost bones.
Echoes rise from well-worn paths,
Wrapping every shadowed laugh.

Moonlit glades where spirits roam,
Weaving memories like a tome.
Threads of magic, soft and clear,
Kiss the heart of all who near.

Crimson leaves and silver skies,
Hold the dreams where wisdom lies.
In the stillness, lore ignites,
Kindling hope on starry nights.

In every nook, secrets cling tight,
Bathed in ethereal delight.
In their presence, we find signs,
Of the magic that entwines.

The Glass Beneath the Moonlit Waves

Underneath the moon's soft gaze,
Glassy depths, a shimmering maze.
Each ripple holds a wistful song,
Calling forth where dreams belong.

Stars reflect in liquid night,
Painting tales of pure delight.
Fish dart through the beams of light,
In this realm, the heart takes flight.

Secrets twirl in tranquil swirls,
Mermaid laughter, boyish whirls.
The water whispers to the shore,
Of hidden worlds and ancient lore.

With each wave, a story spins,
In the depths where silence wins.
Fables gleam in twilight's glow,
Beneath the waves, each echo flows.

In this glass, a moment's grace,
Lost in time, a sacred space.
The moonlight bathes the ocean's song,
An invitation to belong.

Dark Treasures of the Sea Bed

In the shadows where silence reigns,
Lies a world of sunken gains.
Chests of gold and jewels bright,
Cradled soft in endless night.

Whispers haunt the currents' race,
Echoes of a bygone place.
Legends linger 'neath the foam,
In the depths, they'll find their home.

Glistening in the midnight deep,
Secrets that the sea does keep.
Faded maps and tales unwind,
In the darkness, treasure's blind.

Storms may rage and waters crash,
Yet hidden riches gleam and flash.
Every pearl, a longing sigh,
In this grave where dreams do lie.

But beware the sirens' song,
Luring sailors to the throng.
For dark treasures can ensnare,
In the sea's cold, endless lair.

Sirens in the Blackened Tide

In the depths where shadows creep,
The sirens sing, their secrets keep.
Voices weaving, soft and sly,
Lure the lost as the moon rides high.

Through tangled reeds, the whispers flow,
In darkened currents, fears bestow.
Swaying gently, night's embrace,
Calls the wanderers to their place.

Beneath the surface, silence hums,
A hidden world where magic drums.
Glimmers faint, like stars that fade,
Drawn to depths where dreams are laid.

Yet beware the shifting tide,
For not all wishes may abide.
A haunting tune, a shimmering guise,
Entangles hearts within their lies.

So heed the call of tempests wild,
For in their wake, the ocean's child.
The sirens' wail, a bitter balm,
In blackened waves, they weave their charm.

Negotiating Shadows Beneath Waves

Where light dissolves and shadows blend,
The ocean's whispers know no end.
Beneath the crest where dreams take flight,
The currents dance, elusive night.

Secrets of the fathomless deep,
In tangled webs, the dark things creep.
Negotiation with the tide,
Is a gamble where phantoms hide.

Echoes linger in the swell,
Tales of woe, and wishes fell.
Ghostly remnants in the foam,
Beneath the waves, they seek a home.

Mermaid's laughter, soft yet brave,
Marks the journey to the grave.
Glimmers gleam like fleeting stars,
In the dark's embrace, there are scars.

Each ripple tells a story lost,
What was gained, and what the cost.
Beneath the surface, we all strive,
To navigate, to feel alive.

A Journey Through Aquatic Dreams

In silent depths where whispers lie,
Aquatic dreams breathe low and high.
Drifting gently, currents sway,
Carrying hearts on their hidden way.

Chronicles of waves' soft sighs,
Rippling tales beneath the skies.
With every splash, a story flows,
In waters blue, where magic glows.

Illusions swim in twilight's veil,
Through shimmering depths, we set sail.
A tapestry of hopes and fears,
Woven gently with silken tears.

Castles rise in liquid light,
Eclipsed by the pull of night.
In each breath, the sea cradles dreams,
Where nothing's ever as it seems.

The journey twists, and we must heed,
The beckoning of the silent creed.
Through aquatic realms, we float, we dive,
In this enchanted world, we thrive.

Overlapping Canopies of Night

In the hush where shadows meet,
Canopies twist in strange retreat.
Overlapping tales the moon weaves,
Harboring magic that never leaves.

Beneath the branches, darkness blooms,
Embracing night as the last light looms.
The stars they whisper, secrets twine,
In the interstices of time.

Cloaked in sable, the night runs deep,
Where lost souls wander, and spirits weep.
With every rustle, a story shared,
In the blackened woods, love declared.

Echoing softly, the willow sighs,
Holding secrets that never dies.
In these woods, we've all once dreamed,
Life entwined, or so it seemed.

So tread with care where shadows play,
For lingering doubts may lead astray.
In overlapping canopies of night,
Magic lingers, just out of sight.

Midnight's Glassy Heart

In the hush of night, the stars gleam bright,
Reflecting dreams, draped in silver light.
A heart of glass, fragile yet bold,
Whispers secrets waiting to unfold.

The moon's soft glow guides the way,
Where shadows dance, and fairies play.
In the silence, magic stirs,
Bound by the dreams that softly purrs.

Fates entwined in twilight's hand,
Journeying through a twilight land.
Each heartbeat echoes the tales untold,
In midnight's glass, forever enfold.

Through labyrinthine thoughts we soar,
Chasing wonders, seeking more.
With every breath, the night confides,
In glassy chambers where hope abides.

Embrace the night, the dreams arise,
Underneath the velvet skies.
For in the dark, the heart can see,
The beauty of all that's yet to be.

Guardians of the Deep Blue

Beneath the waves, in depths profound,
Where whispered secrets drift around.
Guardians dwell, both fierce and wise,
Their truths concealed in azure skies.

Coral castles rise and fall,
Echoes of a long-lost call.
Creatures of the sea glide by,
Beneath the watchful, knowing sky.

Mysteries twine in currents run,
Veiled in shadows, kissed by sun.
Each ripple tells a tale of old,
In the realm where wonders unfold.

A siren's song, both sweet and deep,
Lures the heart from tranquil sleep.
Will you heed or turn away,
From guardians waiting in the spray?

In depths unknown, there lies a spark,
The heart of ocean, fierce and dark.
A line that binds the safe and free,
Forever shaped by the deep blue sea.

The Allure of the Enigmatic

In shadows cast by candlelight,
Lies the charm of the night's delight.
Whispers wrapped in mystery's lace,
The heart quickens to this embrace.

Secrets linger like the mist,
A fleeting touch, a fleeting kiss.
Curiosity beckons with its caress,
Urging the brave, the bold, no less.

Through veils of dusk, the secrets scheme,
A spellbound world that teems with dream.
Each glance reveals a vivid hue,
In the glance of the unknown, the vivid true.

The flicker of hope, a shiver of dread,
The dance of thoughts where few have tread.
For every question, a thousand more,
In the labyrinth's heart, adventure's core.

Deep in the stillness, stories arise,
Crafted beneath the watchful skies.
To chase the mystery is to live,
In the allure of the enigmatic, we forgive.

Murmurs of the Lost Abyss

In the void where silence reigns,
Lost whispers echo through the chains.
Abyss waits with a patient sigh,
Holding secrets neither low nor high.

Each murmur dances 'neath the waves,
In shadowed depths, where nothing saves.
Time slips through with silent grace,
Painting trails in the darkest space.

Eternal hymns of unseen shores,
In every sound, a yearning pours.
The call of depths we cannot see,
Revealing tales of what could be.

Drifting souls in twilight's hush,
Stirred by wonder, hearts in rush.
Though lost, they weave through night's embrace,
To share their stories, trace by trace.

In every breath, the abyss shall sing,
Of forgotten tales and things that cling.
For in the dark, the light shall form,
Murmurs of the lost, a gentle balm.

Enchantment of the Black Glass

In the depths where shadows creep,
Whispers of the ancients seep.
Fragments of forgotten dreams,
Wrapped in mystery, it seems.

Mirrors hold a secret glance,
Echoes of a timeless dance.
Onyx surfaces await the touch,
A spark of magic, oh, so much.

Glimmers flicker, shadows play,
In the night, gods seem to sway.
With every breath, a story spins,
Of lost loves and hidden sins.

Gaze into the endless night,
Feel the pull of forbidden light.
A cursed wish, a heart's delight,
Bound by fate, an endless flight.

So tread carefully, my friend,
For here, the lines of time may bend.
In the glass, the world will bend,
Magic woven with each tend.

Beneath the Night's Embrace

Under velvet skies we roam,
In the stillness, far from home.
Stars like diamonds, soft and bright,
Guide us through the tender night.

Moonbeams cast their silver glow,
Whispers from the winds that flow.
In the shadows, secrets lie,
Beneath the veil of the midnight sky.

Cloaked in dreams of silent song,
Where the lost and brave belong.
Sighs of longing fill the air,
In this space, we shed our care.

Every heartbeat shares a tale,
Weaving magic, soft and frail.
Secrets linger, breath of fate,
As we dance, we celebrate.

Hold me close, oh, night divine,
Under stars that intertwine.
In the quiet, souls unite,
Bound forever, lost in night.

Secrets of the Starlit Waters

Crystalline waters softly flow,
Reflecting dreams that ebb and grow.
Underneath the moon’s embrace,
Secrets linger, find their place.

Ripples carry tales of old,
Of shipwrecked hearts and treasures told.
In the depths, where silence reigns,
Whispers echo, veiled in pains.

Moonlit paths, a guiding thread,
Lured by voices of the dead.
Mirrored surfaces, glassy gleams,
Unlock the doors of ancient dreams.

Let the currents pull you near,
Gather fragments without fear.
In the starlit waters deep,
Lost are the secrets we keep.

With each tide, a story's spun,
Of battles lost, and victories won.
Heed the call of waters wide,
For in their depths, the past must bide.

Echoes in the Silent Deep

In the stillness, shadows blend,
Where the light and dark descend.
Echoes whisper, soft and low,
In the silent deep, our fates flow.

Resonance of a time gone by,
Where dreams dissolve and spirits sigh.
Irresistible is the pull,
To the depths, so vast, so full.

Beneath the surface, secrets hum,
Melodies of what once was done.
Dancing shadows weave their lore,
Calling out for something more.

Time stands still in this vast sea,
A tapestry of you and me.
Feel the magic in the air,
As we linger, lost in care.

Hear the echoes, soft and sweet,
In the depths where heartbeats meet.
Hold this moment, let it seep,
In the magic of the deep.

Dance of the Sirens in the Dark

In shadows deep where secrets hide,
The sirens sing, their voices glide.
With whispers cool like silver streams,
They call to hearts, igniting dreams.

A flicker of light, a glimmer of hope,
Where the night is rich, and the wild waters mope.
Dance with the waves, let the currents sweep,
In the embrace of the dark, lose not your sleep.

Echoes linger where moonbeams weave,
In the stillness, they taunt and tease.
Mysteries wrapped in velvet night,
A waltz of shadow, a fleeting sight.

With every heartbeat, the tides respond,
A rhythm shared far beyond the pond.
The depths below hold stories untold,
Of love, of loss, of hearts made bold.

So join the dance, let your spirit roam,
With sirens singing, you're never alone.
In twilight's clutch, find solace sweet,
In the dance of the dark, find your heartbeat.

Ghosts of the Ocean's Depths

Beneath the veil of water's sheen,
Whispers call of places unseen.
Ghostly shadows swim and sway,
In moonlit realms where dreams drift away.

Echoes of sailors lost in time,
Mermaids croon their haunting rhyme.
Drifting softly like a tide,
In depths where ancient tales abide.

A shipwrecked love, a treasure's lore,
The ocean keeps what we ignore.
With every wave, a tale is spun,
Of battles fought and songs begun.

From coral tombs to caverns dark,
The ghosts of time leave their mark.
They dance in silence, shadows cast,
In twilight's glow, their whispers last.

Hear them murmur in the deep,
In ocean's heart, the secrets keep.
For every wave that breaks and crests,
The ghostly stories build their nests.

The Charcoal Tides of Tranquility

In shades of grey where waters meet,
The charcoal tides hum soft and sweet.
A canvas brushed by calmest hands,
Where silence reigns on timeless sands.

Once fierce and wild, now still they sway,
In tranquil depths where thoughts can play.
Ripples dance with whispered grace,
In meditative, sacred space.

The horizon blushes, the stars align,
Where dreams are spun, and hearts entwine.
In twilight's hush, let worries flee,
In ocean's arms, find your spree.

Embrace the dark, let shadows guide,
The charcoal tides now open wide.
In every ebb and subtle flow,
Seek peace within, let your spirit grow.

At dawn's first light, let colors bloom,
In tranquil waves dispel the gloom.
With charcoal tides, find harmony,
And dance with waves in ecstasy.

Underwater Chronicles of the Night

In a world where silence reigns supreme,
The underwater tales begin to gleam.
Each current holds a whispered word,
Stories sung, yet rarely heard.

Glimmers of light flicker and pulse,
Beneath the waves, the rhythms convulse.
In the faded glow of midnight's veil,
The chronicles breathe, the echoes sail.

Creatures dance in the lunar glow,
With secrets locked in depths below.
They weave their tales in salt and foam,
In ocean's heart, they find their home.

Ancient songs from long ago,
In shadows where the currents flow.
With every wave, a tale retold,
Of bravery, love, and dreams of gold.

So dive beneath the surface fine,
In the night, let your spirit shine.
For underwater tales wait patiently,
In the embrace of tides, you'll find your key.

Secrets of the Forgotten Reef

Beneath the waves where shadows creep,
A world of wonders, secrets deep.
Coral castles, lost in time,
Whispers of the ocean's rhyme.

Glimmering scales of fish so bright,
Dance through the currents, a splendid sight.
Echoing songs from depths below,
Calling to those who seek to know.

Ancient stories in sands concealed,
Mysteries waiting to be revealed.
Tales of shipwrecks, treasures lost,
Guarded by tides at any cost.

Caves of pearl and shadows long,
Nature's beauty, fierce and strong.
In twilight's glow and morning's beam,
The reef unveils its timeless dream.

So dive with courage, hearts so free,
Embrace the secrets of the sea.
For in the depths, where few may tread,
Lie whispers of the tales long dead.

Haunting Melodies of the Deep

In twilight's gloom, the waters sigh,
A haunting song that sails on high.
Notes from the depths touch every soul,
Entwined in mysteries, making whole.

The sirens call from rocky shores,
Luring dreamers to the ocean's doors.
With every wave, a story spun,
A timeless dance, forever begun.

Choruses rise with the pull of the tide,
Echoing dreams where secrets hide.
In the moon's embrace, shadows play,
Waltzing through night, they fade away.

Melodies drift like whispers soft,
Carried by currents, rising aloft.
In whispers and tides, they speak to thee,
The haunting melodies of the deep sea.

So listen close, let the music call,
To depths of wonder, to rise and fall.
For each note holds a memory sweet,
A journey awaits in the ocean's heartbeat.

Beneath the Tidal Veil

Beyond the reach of sunlit beams,
Where shadowy wonders stir in dreams.
The tidal veil, a shroud of grace,
Hides everything in a secret space.

Creatures roam in tranquil dance,
Casting spells with each happenstance.
Bubbles float like thoughts untold,
Echoes of magic, ancient and bold.

Anemones sway in a rhythmic tide,
In the stillness where secrets reside.
The whispers of pearls and grains of sand,
Form tales woven by the ocean's hand.

In caverns dark and kelp-lined halls,
The spirit of adventure calls.
With every wave, a story brews,
A canvas painted in vibrant hues.

So delve into the mysteries wide,
Under the tidal veil, let dreams abide.
For in the depths, true worlds emerge,
A place where shadows and wonders surge.

Black Glass Beneath the Sea Foam

Where frothy waves kiss sand so fine,
Lies black glass glistening, pure and divine.
Fragments of dreams, washed by the tide,
Whispers of journeys that once would glide.

Waves crash softly, a lullaby sweet,
As sunlight dances on shadows discreet.
Reflecting stories from ages past,
In currents, the memories linger fast.

A treasure unearthed from depths unknown,
In each glimmer, a heart's soft tone.
With every roll, the ocean bestows,
The gifts of time where the wild wind blows.

So stoop and gather, the shards of the sea,
A mosaic of moments, wild and free.
For every piece is a part of the tale,
Of black glass treasures beneath the veil.

So listen closely as the sea speaks,
In whispers of wonder, for knowledge seeks.
In the heart of the foam, memory's echo,
Breathes life anew, in shimmering glow.

The Veil Between Sea and Stone

In twilight's glow, the waves confer,
A song of secrets, soft and pure.
The stones akin to watchful eyes,
Where whispers weave and shadows rise.

An ocean mist, a gentle sigh,
Hides tales of ships that passed by.
The sea holds depth, a hidden throne,
Where dreams and memories overgrown.

Through tides that swell, the currents churn,
With every ebb, more stories yearn.
The stones, they thrum with life's refrain,
A chorus lost, but not in vain.

When starlit skies drape night in blue,
The sea sings melodies anew.
Each wave that breaks, a soft embrace,
Reminds the heart of time and space.

So linger near this sacred shore,
Where sea and stone forevermore
Will whisper truths in rhythmic time,
A lullaby, a perfect rhyme.

Black Stones Whisper to the Current

Black stones rest on the ocean floor,
Guarding secrets forevermore.
They murmur low beneath the tide,
In silent vows, their tales abide.

The current weaves through darkened dreams,
Where starlight fades and twilight gleams.
Each ripple carries ancient lore,
Of sailors lost, of distant shore.

With shadows cast by moon's embrace,
The stones reveal their hidden grace.
As whispers curl in waters deep,
They hold the sorrows that weep and sleep.

Beneath the vault of midnight's gaze,
They call to bring us through the haze.
A symphony of dark and light,
Where echoes dance in endless night.

So heed the whispers that arise,
From blackened stones where truth lies.
In currents wild, their voices blend,
A haunting song that will not end.

Sirens' Lament in Dark Waters

In shadows deep, where kelp entwines,
The sirens sing of past designs.
Their voices flow like silver streams,
Enticing hearts with haunting dreams.

Lonely echoes, their tears unshed,
Drown in the songs of those who've fled.
For every note a life once lost,
They mourn the price, no matter the cost.

Their melodies weave through currents swift,
A bittersweet and gentle gift.
From depths below, their tales arise,
To lure the brave, to curse the wise.

Yet in their chorus, pain remains,
Of sailors drawn to darkened chains.
With every chord, their sorrow flows,
Through tides of time, the heartache grows.

So listen close, when night descends,
To sirens' cries, the voice of friends.
In darkened waters, they lament,
The love they lost, the lives they spent.

The Enigma of Beneath the Surface

Beneath the waves, a world concealed,
In shadows deep, where truths revealed.
The surface shimmers, calm and bright,
Yet hides a realm beyond our sight.

Coral gardens bloom in silence,
Guarding secrets with such defiance.
The creatures glide through liquid dreams,
In patterns soft as moonlit beams.

What wonders lie in depths so wide?
An ancient magic they abide.
Each ripple tells of tales forlorn,
Of battles fought and hearts reborn.

The ocean swells with whispered lore,
In every wave, an opened door.
To dive within, a reckless thought,
Yet in that plunge, pure wisdom's wrought.

So seek the truth beneath the foam,
In every heartbeat, find a home.
For under the surface, mysteries wait,
In depths of blue, we navigate.

Siren Song in a Shattered Shell

In a shell lay a whisper, soft and sweet,
Calling sailors with a haunting beat.
Echoes of laughter float on the breeze,
Wrapped in a shimmer beneath the seas.

Glistening tides, where shadows play,
Lure the heart to a watery sway.
Crimson lips that part with a sigh,
A melody woven, a lover's cry.

Yet beware the depths where secrets swirl,
A jagged stone in an ocean pearl.
For beauty hides where darkness calls,
An echoing laughter as a siren falls.

In crumbling shells, the stories dwell,
Of gales and ships lost, and a distant bell.
A tune that dances through moonlit nights,
Awakens the dreams of ocean flights.

So heed the song, but keep your soul,
For waves can claim what they cannot control.
And in the currents of a longing heart,
One man’s journey may tear apart.

Dark Waves Over Silent Shores

Dark waves roll in with a deepening sigh,
Over silent shores where the shadows lie.
Nighttime whispers in a ghostly tone,
Echoing secrets the sea has sown.

The moon hangs low, casting silvered beams,
On restless waters where silence dreams.
Shattered shells tell tales of the past,
Of promises broken, of treasures cast.

Starlit skies wrap the world in a shroud,
Where whispers of sea life drift through the crowd.
Yet in stillness, a tempest may rise,
As dark waves gather beneath watchful eyes.

Beneath the surface, where shadows creep,
Lie the wishes that the waves keep.
A yearning for light in a world so vast,
Whispers of futures entwined with the past.

So walk with caution on silken sands,
For the ocean knows the heart's demands.
With dark waves crashing, heed their song,
For silent shores can guide you wrong.

The Stone Beneath the Waves

A stone buried deep in an ocean bed,
Holds the dreams of the water said.
Every ripple tells tales of yore,
Of mermaids dancing on a sandy floor.

In the depths where the currents weave,
Mysteries linger, waiting to leave.
Whispers of tides that gently brush,
Against the stone in a languid hush.

When the tides rise, it starts to glow,
Illuminating secrets that flow below.
Echoing laughter of creatures rare,
That sing of love in the salty air.

Yet stones can crumble, as time will show,
And all that once was fades into woe.
But still the tide, with its surging might,
Holds the stone fast through day and night.

So listen closely to the waves' soft song,
For the stories beneath are never wrong.
In the silence below, a truth prevails,
Tales of love and loss told in sighs and gales.

Mysteries of the Deepening Tide

The mysteries lie where the deep tide swells,
In shadows where the ocean dwells.
With every wave that crashes high,
A story unfolds beneath the sky.

Echoes of whispers, a mermaid's tune,
Drift through the currents beneath the moon.
Tangled in weeds, a treasure rests,
Guarded by secrets, time's gentle tests.

Legends entwined in the sea's embrace,
Where time stands still and dreams interlace.
The pull of the tide tells tales of old,
Of hidden realms and hearts turned bold.

Yet the depth is vast, and the light is faint,
Where sorrow mingles with wishful paint.
In the ebb and flow of darkened waves,
Lie the tales of the brave and the knaves.

So wander the shores where the sea meets sand,
And listen to whispers from a timeless strand.
For the mysteries of the ocean's tide,
Are waiting to share what they'd kept inside.

Veils of Night Above Aquatic Realms

In the depths where shadows creep,
Veils of night in silence weep.
Whispers wrap the water's glow,
Secrets dance in ebb and flow.

Fish like specters glide in dreams,
Underneath the moon's soft beams.
Currents sing a lullaby,
As stars in darkened waters lie.

Bubbles rise like thoughts unspoken,
Vows of old and hearts still broken.
The silence of the ocean's heart,
Holds the tales that drift apart.

Shapes of light, like ancient lore,
Reveal what lies on ocean's floor.
With every wave, a story's spun,
Beneath the watchful eyes of sun.

When the tide begins to sway,
Night will guide the dreams astray.
In the realms where shadows roam,
The ocean calls us back to home.

Moonlit Drift of Spirit Stones

Above the waves, the moon casts light,
Guiding stones through endless night.
Whispers swirl on silver tides,
Ancient spirits, our trusted guides.

Crystals gleam with an otherworldly grace,
Reflecting dreams, lost in space.
Every ripple, a story told,
Of destinies intertwined and bold.

Drifting softly, the night unfolds,
Embracing secrets the ocean holds.
In the depths, past shadows deep,
The spirit stones in silence keep.

With each wave, the tides do sway,
Guiding souls who've lost their way.
Moonlit paths of dreams once known,
Lead us to the realms we've sown.

Together, in this mystic trance,
We find ourselves in ocean's dance.
As waves unite the hearts of stone,
We drift on currents of the unknown.

The Glistening Shards of Fate

Shards of fate upon the shore,
Glisten brightly, tales of yore.
Each fragment tells a tale untold,
Of paths chosen and dreams so bold.

Bathed in light of dawn's embrace,
They shimmer with a timeless grace.
Whispers call from distant lands,
As destiny entwines our hands.

In the quiet, secrets gleam,
Fragments of a broken dream.
Bound by threads of joy and sorrow,
Shards of fate lead to tomorrow.

Rainbows arch in skies above,
Promising a world of love.
With each step, we pave the way,
To bright tomorrows from today.

In the sunlight's gentle glow,
We gather shards, let stories flow.
With open hearts, we take our place,
In the dance of time and space.

Chasing Illusions in Midnight Waters

Beneath the stars, illusions play,
In midnight waters, dreams stray.
Ghostly figures swirl and twine,
Reflections of what could be mine.

Chasing shadows through the night,
Hopes alight on waves so bright.
Every ripple, a promise made,
In darkness, secrets never fade.

The water's surface holds the truth,
Of youthful dreams and fleeting youth.
With every glance, a new disguise,
In the depths, reality lies.

Time flows softly, swift as breath,
In the stillness lies life and death.
As we chase what we hold dear,
Midnight whispers draw us near.

Yet in the heart of midnight's sighs,
Illusions fade, but hope still flies.
With dawn's first light, we may reclaim,
The essence of our whispered names.

Midnight Reflections on the Shore

The moonlight dances on the tide,
Whispering secrets of the night.
Waves caress the grainy sand,
In the dark, the world feels right.

Stars above twinkle like dreams,
Casting their glow on a restless sea.
The wind carries tales from afar,
Inviting us to set our spirits free.

Footprints trace where we have wandered,
Leaving marks on the silken shore.
Each step a story, softly pondered,
Reminders of what we adore.

The tide pulls back, then rushes in,
In its rhythm, life's dance unfolds.
We find our peace amidst the chaos,
As the ocean's heart gently holds.

Tides of time will ebb and flow,
Yet the memories will remain.
On this shore, where dreams are sewn,
Our souls entwined, forever gain.

Beneath the Siren's Veil

In waters deep where shadows linger,
The sirens sing, their voices sweet.
Sirens lure with fingers beckoning,
Tales of old in each heartbeat.

Cloaked in mist and moonlit shimmer,
The depths below hold secrets tight.
With every note, the waves grow dimmer,
Guiding hearts into the night.

A melody of longing whispers,
Calling those who dare to dive.
In the embrace of their soft splendor,
Souls are lost, yet feel alive.

Glistening fins and eyes like midnight,
Sparkle through the curtain of foam.
They weave enchantments, pure delight,
In the depths, where wonders roam.

Yet beware the shadows lurking,
Beneath the song’s hypnotic sway.
For every tune that leaves us yearning,
Hides a tale of hidden prey.

Shadows of the Enchanted Lagoon

In a lagoon where night blooms bright,
Shadows dance in soft embrace.
Magic whispers on gossamer wings,
Filling the air with a thrilling grace.

Moonbeams glide on shimmering waters,
Reflecting dreams that come and go.
Each ripple tells a forgotten story,
Of lovers kissed by the twilight's glow.

Will-o'-the-wisps in playful flitter,
Guide the lost to the heart's true song.
Nature's laughter, a gentle Twitter,
Where souls reborn find they belong.

Trees stand guard like ancient sages,
Whispering secrets to the night.
In the soft embrace of their branches,
We lose ourselves in pure delight.

With every shadow cast and flicker,
Lies a promise of tales untold.
In the lagoon where dreams grow thicker,
Magic lives, as hearts unfold.

Eclipsed Echoes of an Ocean Dream

When twilight falls, the sea turns dark,
A silken shroud, where dreams take flight.
Echoes of laughter linger, stark,
In the embrace of the endless night.

Waves retreat, leaving hushed whispers,
Footsteps trace the edges of time.
Beneath the stars, a world unfurls,
Where each moment is pure and sublime.

The horizon bleeds in colors unseen,
Crimson and indigo blend in one.
A canvas painted in hues between,
The family of night and day, undone.

Figures dance in the silver light,
While the ocean hums a sacred tune.
Lost in the magic of this twilight,
Hearts entwined beneath the moon.

But all must fade; the shadows beckon,
As dawn awakens with gentle sighs.
Yet the echoes of dreams, we reckon,
Will always linger in the skies.

Sirens Beneath the Stormy Skies

Beneath the clouds, in shadows deep,
The sirens call, their secrets keep.
With voices soft as gentle breeze,
They lure the hearts and minds with ease.

The tempest roars, the ocean cries,
Yet in their song, a truth defies.
Through thunder's clash and lightning's dance,
They weave a tale, a timeless romance.

These echoes linger, through night's embrace,
Inviting wanderers to lose their grace.
To follow dreams where waves collide,
And find their fate on ocean's tide.

Beware the pull, the deepening swell,
For not all tales are fit to tell.
The sky may darken, the night may sprawl,
Yet still they sing, enchanting all.

In storms they thrive, in whispers loud,
The sirens dance in shadows proud.
With every note, a world unfurled,
Under the stormy skies, they twirled.

The Depths of Midnight Secrets

In quiet depths where darkness dwells,
The midnight secrets weave their spells.
With whispered thoughts that softly stray,
They guide the lost, then fade away.

Among the shadows, stories dwell,
In watery caverns, time will tell.
Of dreams once bright, now cloaked in night,
Their haunting truths, a fleeting sight.

The moonlight glimmers on hidden fears,
Reflecting hopes, and long-lost tears.
In mystery wrapped, all wishes sleep,
Beneath the waves, their silence deep.

Yet every glance at starlit skies,
Will spark the flame of spirits wise.
They whisper words, both near and far,
And guide the way to who we are.

For in the dark, there lies a spark,
A flicker bright against the stark.
Embrace the night, let shadows play,
In depths of secrets, find your way.

Luminous Stones on an Untamed Coast

Upon the shore where wild waves crash,
Luminous stones in moonlit flash.
They twinkle bright, a sight to see,
Whispers of ancient mystery.

The ocean breathes, a rhythmic song,
With every tide, where dreams belong.
They tell of tales from ages past,
In shimmering light, their shadows cast.

Each stone a story, each glow a voice,
An invitation to make a choice.
To wander forth, to seek delight,
Along the coast, through endless night.

The winds do howl, the storms may rage,
Yet here the stones unveil their page.
Of daring souls who braved the sea,
To find their place, to simply be.

So gather forth, let wonders guide,
These luminous stones, our constant tide.
Embrace the wild, the untamed quest,
And find within, your heart's own rest.

Whispers of the Aquatic Night

In the stillness of the tranquil deep,
Where secrets play and shadows seep,
The whispers weave a tale so rare,
Of life concealed beneath the glare.

With moonlight soft that blankets all,
They dance in dreams, the tides enthrall.
The night unveils, through ripples slow,
The hidden paths that currents flow.

In currents swirling, voices blend,
With lullabies that never end.
For every wave, a spark of fate,
In liquid tales, where dreams await.

The world above, a distant haze,
While down below, the water plays.
In gentle sways, their secrets lie,
A lullaby beneath the sky.

So listen close to the watery sound,
For in each note, the heart is found.
In whispers soft, beneath the light,
Awaits the magic of the night.

Tides of Time and Starlight

Waves that whisper secrets old,
In the moonlight's gentle gold,
Each ripple carries tales untold,
Of hearts that brave the night so bold.

Stars like diamonds in the sea,
Shimmering with quiet glee,
They hold the dreams that dare to fly,
In realms where lost souls softly sigh.

Time flows with a fluid grace,
In this enchanted, timeless place,
Where shadows dance and echoes play,
And wishes wander far away.

The currents weave our destinies,
In the land of faded memories,
As visions fade and dawn takes flight,
I chase the fading spark of light.

So let the tide bear me away,
To where the stars and oceans sway,
In the embrace of night divine,
I'll sail the seas of fate, in time.

Beneath the Surface's Lullaby

The ocean sings a soothing tune,
Softly draping the afternoon,
Where dreamers rest in watery beds,
And drift on currents, wake their heads.

Kelp like curtains sways and glows,
In gentle swirls, where silence grows,
The shimm'ring fish, a fleeting flash,
In shadows deep, their secrets thrash.

Beneath the waves, the world keeps still,
In whispers curled, a hidden thrill,
The shimmered shells tell tales of yore,
As tides weave stories evermore.

With every swell, my thoughts take flight,
Entwined in dreams like stars at night,
And here I find my tranquil song,
In currents deep, where I belong.

For every wave a lullaby,
That cradles hearts beneath the sky,
In rippling peace, we softly glide,
Beneath the sea, where dreams abide.

The Allure of Twilight's Abyss

As daylight fades to dusk's embrace,
The twilight whispers of its grace,
In hues of orange, gold, and blue,
Where secrets dance, and shadows grew.

The horizon melts, a canvas vast,
With fleeting moments that slip past,
Each echo calling to the night,
With promise wrapped in starlit light.

In the silence, a tendril tight,
The enchanting pull of shade and light,
Where dreams and desires intertwine,
In the silent depths of the divine.

Through veils of dusk, I wander free,
To the land of mystery, I flee,
Among the stars that gently gleam,
In the embrace of twilight's dream.

This allure holds me in its thrall,
A spell that beckons, entices all,
In twilight's arms, I'll find my way,
In the abyss, where shadows play.

Echoes of the Deep Blue Heart

In the depths where silence reigns,
Whispers linger, soft refrains,
The ocean hums a timeless song,
Echoes of love where I belong.

Each wave a pulse, a rhythmic beat,
A dance of souls, both cool and sweet,
With salty tears of joys and pains,
In every crest, in every wanes.

The blue heart beats, so deep, so strong,
In currents' flow, where we belong,
Where memories are etched in foam,
And ancient tales, like ocean roam.

As shadows fade and daylight breaks,
The echoes blend with morning wakes,
A tapestry of love's embrace,
In the deep blue's warm, eternal space.

So let the sea cradle the night,
Under the veil of soft starlight,
For in this heart, forever be,
Echoes of lost infinity.

Siren's Shadows on Midnight Waters

In the quiet hush of twilight's song,
Siren whispers call, where shadows belong.
Rippling waters with silvered light,
A dance of spirits, in the deep of night.

Glimmers of laughter, like stars they gleam,
Echoes of longing in a haunting dream.
Beneath the moon's gaze, secrets unfold,
The tales of the deep, both mysterious and bold.

Waves cradle whispers of souls gone by,
Siren’s embrace, a sweet lullaby.
Heartbeats entwined in the melody's sway,
Lost in the depths, where shadows play.

Through tangled kelp and silken sea foam,
She beckons the weary to leave their home.
With promises woven in shimmering strands,
A world that awaits in enchanted lands.

Oh, sailor beware, as you drift on the tide,
For the siren's sweet song is a treacherous guide.
Yet in her embrace, one might find the light,
In the dance of shadows on midnight's flight.

The Art of Evasive Depths

Beneath the surface where silence reigns,
The art of evasion, a dance with chains.
Currents are secrets that twist and turn,
Each flicker of light, a lesson to learn.

In the corners of depths, where shadows creep,
Whispers of the ancients lull those to sleep.
A flick of a fin, a ripple so sly,
A magical silence that holds a soft sigh.

Gone are the hopes, beneath the vast waves,
Where longing and sorrow intertwine like knaves.
Evasive the heart that seeks the unknown,
In the embrace of depths, forever alone.

Colors unfathomed, a mystical ballet,
Where creatures of wonder dance night and day.
They weave and they wind, like thoughts unexpressed,
In the art of the deep, where souls find their rest.

Through the murk and the mist, a call can be felt,
In the quiet of depth where mysteries melt.
So dive into shadows, let the currents intertwine,
And feel the allure of the art so divine.

Lament of the Submerged Stones

In the stillness of depths, where echoes reside,
The submerged stones hold stories inside.
Whispers of anguish, lost tales of yore,
Each grain of sand speaks of life's endless lore.

Trapped in their silence, they yearn to be free,
Witness to waves and the shadows of glee.
Caught in the currents, their voices grow faint,
A lament for the dreams that they never could paint.

Through tempest and tide, their spirits remain,
Guarding the secrets of joy and of pain.
As the water flows over, their memories swell,
A tribute to life, to love's fragile spell.

Once they were mountains, proud, tall and wide,
Now they're mere whispers beneath the white tide.
Each lapping wave carries a piece of the past,
In the lament of stones, as memories cast.

So listen in stillness, be gentle and kind,
For the submerged stones have stories entwined.
They sing of the lives where the sun used to shine,
A lament for the echoes, forever divine.

Bewitched by the Night's Embrace

Enchanted by whispers when twilight awakes,
The night drapes its cloak, while the silence breaks.
Moonlight dances softly on waters so still,
With shadows that glide like dreams, they fulfill.

Stars sprinkle magic on waves gently crest,
While the world holds its breath, in the night's sweet rest.
Each shadow a secret, each glimmer a trace,
As we float in the magic, bewitched by grace.

Voices of nightfall hum low in the air,
A melody sweet, a lover's soft prayer.
Cradled in darkness, where dreams never cease,
In the night's embrace, every heart finds peace.

Every ripple fascinates, every hush reveals,
The art of the night and the how it feels.
With stars as our witnesses, and the moon as our guide,
We're spellbound by shadows along the dark tide.

So let us wander through this magical space,
Forever enchanted in night's warm embrace.
For in every heartbeat, a story is laid,
In the bewitching darkness, where dreams are made.

The Cursed Reflection of the Abyss

In shadows deep, where whispers dwell,
A mirror gleams, a ghostly spell.
It shows the past, the fears we hide,
A cursed depth where secrets bide.

Each gaze reveals a heart's despair,
Promises lost, beyond repair.
In silent screams, the echoes play,
A dance of dreams that fade away.

The water churns with tales untold,
Of shattered hopes and hearts grown cold.
A haunting song of sorrow's grace,
Reflects the truth we can’t erase.

Yet through the dark, a flicker glows,
A chance to change what fate bestows.
With courage found, we start anew,
And shatter chains that bind us too.

So peer once more, with eyes unshut,
Release the past from heavy strut.
Embrace the light, the bonds that mend,
For from the abyss, hope shall ascend.

Tides of Elysian Enchantment

When moonlight spills on tranquil seas,
And whispers ride the gentle breeze,
The shores of dreams begin to shine,
In waves adorned with starlit wine.

Each tide that laps against the sand,
Carries a wish, a lover's hand.
Elysian shores where spirits play,
And dance beneath the dawn's bright ray.

With shells that sing of magic dust,
In every grain, a spark of trust.
The ocean's heart beats strong and true,
In tides of enchantment, we find anew.

So splash and twirl in waters deep,
Where echoes of our dreams won’t sleep.
In every wave, a tale unfolds,
Of love, of laughter, and of gold.

As stars align in night's embrace,
And time weaves on with timeless grace,
We ride the tides that never cease,
In Elysium, find our peace.

Castles of Stone Beneath the Waves

Beneath the foam, in twilight's grasp,
Lie castles grand, in silken clasp.
Their towers rise, like dreams of old,
In tales of mermaids, brave and bold.

The sea will guard their ancient reign,
With treasures lost and hidden gain.
Each stone a whisper, soft and clear,
Of seafarers who held them dear.

In moonlit nights, their shadows loom,
A mystic air, a sense of doom.
Yet in their halls, the laughter stays,
In ghosts that dance in watery bays.

The current cradles secrets deep,
In dreams that wander and never sleep.
With coral crowns and sapphire light,
These castles sing of pure delight.

So if you dare to dive below,
And trace the paths where memories flow,
You'll find the heart of ocean's throne,
In castles built of stone, alone.

Echoes of a Celestial Tide

In twilight's glow, when stars align,
The ocean hums a tune divine.
Each wave a brushstroke, soft and bright,
A canvas kissed by velvet night.

Echoes rise from depths unknown,
Where secrets stir, and dreams are sown.
They call to hearts both near and far,
As constellations paint the shore.

The lunar pull, it draws us near,
To cosmic tales, both sweet and clear.
In rhythms of the endless sea,
We find our place, where we are free.

With each soft splash, a story flows,
Of love that sparks and brightly glows.
In every tide, a wish takes flight,
Echoes ring through the quiet night.

So listen close, for in the swell,
The universe has much to tell.
In every heartbeat, every sigh,
The celestial tide will never die.

Inked Currents of Ancient Lore

In quiet glades where whispers flow,
The ink of ages starts to glow.
Each droplet tells of battles won,
And secrets kept from everyone.

Beneath the trees, the shadows dance,
A tapestry of fleeting chance.
With every stroke, a tale is spun,
Of heroes lost and legends run.

The parchment crinkles, time stands still,
A world reborn by writer's quill.
In silence deep, the ink does gleam,
As echoes bend into a dream.

With whispered words, the story weaves,
A thread of fate that never leaves.
An ancient script in moonlight shines,
Reviving hearts through careful lines.

Each tale a journey, fierce and bright,
Through darkness deep, toward morning light.
Together bound, both past and new,
Inked currents drifting ever true.

Tales from the Deep Sea Night

In waters dark where secrets dwell,
The ocean's lullaby does swell.
A dance of shadows, soft and grand,
A symphony from ocean's hand.

Moonlit waves in silver churn,
With every crest, a heart will yearn.
Beneath the surface, myths arise,
Where sirens sing and dreams disguise.

The compass spins in endless tide,
Adventure calls from far and wide.
With every splash, the echoes ring,
Of whispered hope the night does bring.

Emerging stories, salty air,
With every howl, they twist and flare.
The tempest roars, yet hearts remain,
Bound to the depths, we break the chain.

Through churning seas, the tales ignite,
A tapestry spun in the night.
With every plunge, the legends soar,
Bold tales from the deep forevermore.

Shadows Whispers of Forgotten Dreams

In twilight's haze where silence breathes,
The shadows weave through autumn leaves.
Forgotten voices softly call,
As time embraces one and all.

With every sigh, the memories swell,
Like hidden pearls in ocean's shell.
The past entwined in twilight's glow,
Is where the secret longings flow.

A flicker here, a phantom there,
In silent halls, the ghosts lay bare.
Their stories blend with starlit skies,
While time, a river, never lies.

Through endless night, the whispers creep,
Awakening tales from timeless sleep.
Each echo holds a lingering trace,
Of dreams that time cannot erase.

As shadows dance with fleeting grace,
In soft embrace, we find our place.
For in the deep of night we glean,
The whispered truths of dreams unseen.

Depths of the Enchanted Abyss

Beneath the waves, where magic flows,
In enchanted realms, the mystery grows.
With every tide, a legend breathes,
In hidden depths where silence weaves.

The colors pulse in shades unknown,
With whispers soft like seeds they've sown.
In coral cradles, stories hide,
Of ancient quests and dreams untried.

As tendrils dance in gentle swirls,
The echoes of forgotten pearls.
In harmony with nature's flow,
The secrets of the deep we know.

Through shimmering light, the creatures glide,
As time slips by, a flowing tide.
In every wave, excitement brews,
As we unleash our inner muse.

In depths swirling with vivid delight,
We explore the magic, dark yet bright.
With every splash, our hearts we confess,
To the depths of the enchanted abyss.

Dusk's Arrival on the Ethereal Waters

The sun bows low, a fiery sphere,
As shadows lengthen, night draws near.
With whispers soft, the waters gleam,
A tranquil heart, a waking dream.

Stars ignite, their silver spark,
Reflecting tales from worlds so dark.
The gentle breeze, a lover's sigh,
Beneath the dusk, the secrets lie.

Mirrored skies in twilight's thrall,
Where silence reigns, and echoes call.
Each ripple holds a story old,
Of distant lands and hearts so bold.

In spectral hues, the night unfolds,
A tapestry of dreams retold.
From shores unknown, the stories drift,
In twilight's arms, our spirits lift.

As shadows dance upon the tide,
In every wave, we seek to hide.
A dance of stars, a soft lament,
Night's gentle grip, the day's content.

The Pitch of Sirens and Shadows

When moonlight weaves through trees like lace,
And whispered fears begin their chase.
The sirens call with haunting grace,
In their embrace, the lost find space.

Through fog and mist, the echoes glide,
Beneath the waters, where dreams reside.
A melody steeped in dark desire,
To chart the depths, we risk the fire.

With shadows mingling in the night,
And fleeting glimpses of eerie light,
We wander far, our spirits bold,
Into the tales of legends told.

Each note a thread in fate’s own weave,
A siren's smile, so hard to leave.
Yet in the pitch, a warning sung,
Of fortunes lost and songs unsung.

In every whisper, danger stirs,
In midnight's breath, a pulse occurs.
As shadows sway and secrets unfurl,
We navigate this mystic world.

Midnight's Gem Among the Depths

Beneath the waves where secrets bloom,
A midnight gem dispels the gloom.
In ocean's cradle, lost and found,
A spark of light beneath the ground.

With shimmered shells and coral red,
The whispers of the ancients thread.
Each current sings, a soothing sound,
In depths of blue where dreams abound.

A treasure trove, where legends sleep,
In silence held, the secrets keep.
With each tide's turn and ebbing flow,
The heart of night begins to glow.

From deep within, a pulse ignites,
A guiding star in shadowed nights.
To seek the truth in watery halls,
Where every echo softly calls.

Emerging bold from depths unseen,
A beacon bright, so pure, so keen.
In midnight's arms, we dive and feel,
The world below, both dark and real.

Tales of Immortal Depths Unspoken

In caverns deep, where silence dwells,
The timeless lore of ocean bells.
With every wave, a tale to tell,
Of dreams and fears in shadow's spell.

They speak of stars that fell from grace,
Of heartache woven in this place.
From sunken ships to ghostly shores,
The ocean breathes, forever roars.

In the twilight's hush, the stories weave,
Things once believed, now hard to conceive.
Where memories linger like a sigh,
In depths profound, where echoes lie.

Each whisper wraps a soul in plight,
As waves caress the cloak of night.
An endless dance of time and tide,
Where myths are born and secrets bide.

Through shadows cast by moonlit beams,
The sea reveals our hopes and dreams.
In immortal depths, unspoken tales,
Guide weary hearts where courage prevails.

The Mermaid's Darkest Lullaby

Beneath the waves where shadows creep,
The mermaid sings her secrets deep.
Her voice a haunting, soft embrace,
In moonlit tides, her fears find space.

A lullaby of ocean's woe,
Where dreams dissolve and sorrows flow.
She hums of love that slips away,
And dances with the dying day.

With silver scales and misty hair,
She weaves a tale of dark despair.
The seaweed sways to her lament,
In depths where light is rarely spent.

Yet in her heart a flicker glows,
A hope that through the current grows.
For even in the darkest night,
The stars above still shine so bright.

So listen close, if you dare dive,
To mermaid dreams that still alive.
For every song of grief and pain,
Contains a spark of love's sweet grain.

Tempest's Jewel of the Deep

In storms where passion reigns so wild,
The ocean's heart is fiercely styled.
A jewel born from thunder's roar,
It glimmers bright on the ocean floor.

The tempest rages, waves collide,
Each crest a memory, each trough a tide.
Yet in the chaos, beauty's found,
In swirling depths where dreams abound.

Emerald waters filled with strife,
Reveal the harshness of the life.
But through the chaos, light will seep,
Transforming struggles into keep.

For pearls arise from grit and tear,
And treasures bloom from deep despair.
So fear not storms that rage and howl,
Embrace the jewel, let hope avowel.

Through tempests fierce, the heart will shine,
With every struggle, love's design.
For in the depths where shadows play,
The jewel of hope will light your way.

The Glistening Abyss

In twilight's glow, the abyss gleams,
A world alive with silent dreams.
Each ripple holds a whispered plea,
To fathom depths of mystery.

The glistening dark, a velvet shroud,
Where secrets linger, soft and proud.
In shadows deep, the lost find rest,
In tranquil waves, their sorrows pressed.

An underwater symphony plays,
In currents smooth, where silence sways.
The coral reefs like jewels hide,
Within the depths, where hearts confide.

But tread with care on ocean's floor,
For beauty dances, evermore.
With every glance, a glance may steal,
The light of day, a fading reel.

The abyss calls with its siren song,
Inviting those who long for wrong.
Yet in its depths, be wary still,
For darkness blooms with gentle thrill.

Shattered Illusions in the Deep Blue

In depths where visions twist and weave,
Illusions shimmer, then deceive.
The ocean's guise, a fickle friend,
A tale of truths that never end.

What glimmers bright may fade to grey,
As currents pull the light away.
An echo lost in fathomless space,
The searching soul must find its place.

With shattered hopes like broken glass,
Reflections bend as moments pass.
Yet every fragment sings a tune,
Of dreams that once ignited June.

For in the blue, where shadows play,
A heart can learn to drift away.
From shattered dreams, new paths will sprout,
In blue's embrace, release your doubt.

So dive into the unknown sea,
Where shattered hopes may set you free.
With every stroke, let courage rise,
And find the beauty in disguise.

Shadows of Midnight on Ocean's Crown

Beneath the cloak of night, so deep,
The ocean whispers secrets, it keeps.
Stars flicker like dreams on a silver sea,
Where shadows dance, wild and free.

Moonlight glimmers on waves that sigh,
A lullaby sung, as time drifts by.
Ghostly tales of sailors lost,
In this twilight realm, a heavy cost.

Echoes of laughter, now but a breath,
In the currents of longing, a silent death.
The crown of water, a throne of pain,
As shadows weave memories like rain.

Glimpses of figures, lost to the tide,
Whirlpools of sorrow where spirits bide.
The vastness calls, both soft and stark,
In the shadows of midnight, there lies a spark.

A journey awaits, through depths yet untold,
In the heart of the ocean, a story unfolds.
To seek the light where darkness reigns,
Is to unearth the truth in these chains.

The Siren's Veil of Stone

In caves of crystal, echoes hum,
The siren’s song, a call to come.
Veiled in shadows, she weaves her threads,
Entrancing hearts, where reason treads.

Lurking just beneath the shore,
The promise of love, yet so much more.
With eyes like stars and a haunting grace,
In her gaze, you lose your place.

Her laughter, a breeze, swift and light,
Turns sweet temptation into night.
In depths of stone, hidden from sight,
She leads you forth, toward endless blight.

Caught in the net, your will undone,
The siren’s game, you’ve lost before begun.
In shadows long, where dreams are sown,
You find your heart in a shell of stone.

Beneath the waves, remembrance wakes,
With every ripple, a promise breaks.
Her veil surrounds, soft as a sigh,
The siren’s world, where shadows lie.

Reflections in the Abyss

Gaze into waters, dark and deep,
Where secrets lie and shadows creep.
Reflections weave a tale of woe,
An abyss where lost souls go.

Beneath the surface, whispers swirl,
In twilight’s grasp, they twist and twirl.
Mirrored faces, yet none to know,
The depth of sorrow, a silent show.

In the hush of night, hope flickers low,
Within the tide, the heart's undertow.
Drawn to the edge, curiosity sparks,
As darkness beckons, it leaves its marks.

Yet still, a shimmer, a glimmering light,
On the brink of despair, hope's fragile fight.
What haunts in shadows may yet reveal,
The truth in the deep, both cold and real.

So peer closely into this abyss,
Where every ripple holds a kiss.
The mirror may break, the waters churn,
In reflections found, lost souls can learn.

Where the Depths Meet Darkness

In silent crevices where shadows merge,
The depths entwine, a haunting surge.
A dance of tides in endless night,
Veils of darkness, holding tight.

Fathoms below, where secrets dwell,
Eldritch whispers weave a spell.
The ocean's breath, a chilling sigh,
As dreams unravel and softly die.

Creatures of legend slink and glide,
In the cradle of darkness, so much to hide.
Each wave that crashes speaks of lore,
In the shadows, they ask for more.

Beneath the moon's soft, silvery glow,
The world above remains unknown.
Where the depths meet darkness, fate awaits,
In the arms of the sea, destiny creates.

Echoes of the past in whispers bleed,
In the abyss of night, every heart is freed.
To find the light in the cloak of despair,
Is to dance with shadows, and leave your care.

www.ingramcontent.com/pod-product-compliance
Ingram Content Group UK Ltd.
Pitfield, Milton Keynes, MK11 3LW, UK
UKHW021439280125
4335UKWH00035B/311

9 781805 638681